Stage Struck

A Manual for Low Tech, Low Cost, High Performance Church, School and Community

Theatricals

Louise Ulmer

ISBN 0-941367-02-9

Copyright 2003

Peach Blossom Publications
136 Centre Line Avenue
Williamsport, Pennsylvania 17701

written by Louise Ulmer
illustrations by Michelle Zapel from originals by Louise Ulmer
.cover picture taken at mall in Niagara Falls, Canada

first edition published by Contemporary Drama Services 1982

for Dean Floyd Clark

Johnson Bible College

who taught drama by allowing us to do it ourselves

with love

OTHER BOOKS BY

Louise Ulmer

ABCs of FOOD, A Study of Food as History, Story,
Tradition and Nutrition

The Four O'clock Mystery

The Globster of Glassy Beach

The Bible that Wouldn't Burn:
How the Tyndale Version of the Bible Came About

Serenade of the South

Winter Shaker

And in the Arch Book Series by Concordia:

What's the Matter With Job?
The Man Who Learned to Give
The Son Who Said He Wouldn't
Elijah and the Wicked Queen
Jesus' Twelve Disciples
Samuel the Judge
Good Friday

Let's Play a Bible Story I and II

Table of Contents

Chapter One: To Dream the Impossible Dream

CHURCH THEATER'S UNIQUE PROBLEMS

The church play director has a handful of problems. Many are those he has in common with all directors and yet, some are uniquely his own.

His first problem is finding a play that will please everybody. It must contain a worthwhile lesson because people come to church to be fed spiritually not just entertained. (This is not bad advice for any director.)

His second hurdle is to be sure there is nothing objectionable in the play. It must not offend anybody by being in poor taste, and it must not consciously or unconsciously lead the audience to accept some teaching contrary to Christianity. Before he gets into hot water, a wise director will discuss any potential problem with the minister. This is not to say that a good play won't step on a few toes the way a good sermon should.

With these two major hitches out of the way, the church director can go on to the usual problems of directing:
1. Can you afford the set and costumes?
2. Do you have enough skilled actors?
3. Is there enough rehearsal time?

Even with these questions settled, the church director may meet another snag before the project is ready for lift-off. He may meet with a lack of enthusiasm. Many a congregation — with good reason — is embarassed about programs they have had to endure in the past. If this is the case, it will be squarely up to you to change that by giving them a show they can be proud of.

For the church play to have a professional look you will have to work like pros. No group of amateurs can give a respectable performance with only a few rehearsals.

This is the secret of being a good director of amateurs. If you are going to direct inexperienced actors, you are going to have to teach a course in acting at the same time. When you are giving instructions to a player who doesn't know "keep your triangles" from "hold for three beats" you will be spending more time explaining acting fundamentals than directing. The solution is simple enough and it is worth its weight in platinum. It is best to hold acting classes several weeks in advance of rehearsals.

Every class you can squeeze in is worth it. Stress the importance of these preliminary classes by explaining how much rehearsal time will be saved by having a knowledge of technique.

Naturally, you can't teach everything in a few sessions, but every little bit is a help. In the acting chapter the bare necessities are included for great actors never stop learning with these basics as their foundation.

No book in the world is a better teacher than experience. Get your class into action doing exercises so they can gain confidence and experience. Acting cannot be learned from a book; acting is learned by acting.

STAGE GEOGRAPHY

Cast and crew should know stage directions and stage areas as second nature.

Naturally, the most important action takes place in the center. Down Center is the most important area of all. It is reserved for the most important players doing their most important actions.

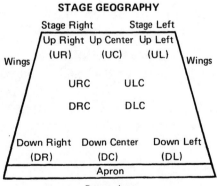

STAGE GEOGRAPHY

Stage Right   Stage Left

Up Right Up Center Up Left
(UR)   (UC)   (UL)

Wings   Wings

URC   ULC

DRC   DLC

Down Right Down Center Down Left
(DR)   (DC)   (DL)

Apron

Proscenium

TRYOUTS AND CASTING

You may think you have so few characters to choose from that holding tryouts is unnecessary, but holding tryouts helps both the director and the players. Players feel they have a better chance at the major roles and directors may be surprised to find some players to be much better than they imagined.

Begin by assigning someone to read each role and put them all onstage to read. Then keep switching them around until you see who looks best in each role. An actor may come to try for one part and be amazed to find out he is superb in a different one.

Right from the beginning, establish the attitude that all roles are important. There is no need for jealousy over the major roles. The biggest part may not be the "best" part. It doesn't matter which role you play but how you play that role you do have. Even a walk-on can be spectacular if their performance is something special. Some of the most memorable performances on stage or screen are made unforgettable by an actor's dazzling performance. Notice the minor players in *Ben Hur* — the old Arab, the deaf mute, the emperor, the lepers, and the blind beggar all give gem performances.

Never turn anybody away. If you have someone who is dying for a part but is outclassed for all the roles, find a place for him by putting him in as an extra. Urge him to work on the crew, too. He will gain invaluable experience and be beneficial to the show in many ways. Never turn down a volunteer. There's no such thing as too many crew workers. You will need all the help you can get and, importantly, the more people you have involved in the production, the more enthusiasm you will generate. The more people there are involved, the more friends and family will come to see their work.

The main thing to remember about casting is how well the actor comes across as the character he is portraying. Some actors simply do not fit certain roles. Still, don't make that judgment without a tryout. You may be amazed how actors you least expect can adapt to parts you wouldn't dream they can play judging by the way they act in everyday life.

```
TRYOUT RATING SHEET

Actor's Name:_____
Description of Actor:_____
Height:   Tall   Average   Short
Size:   Small   Average   Large
Unusual physical characteristics:_____

_____
Character:_____
Character Desription:_____
Height:   Tall   Average   Short   Irrelevant
Unusual physical characteristics:_____

_____
Speaking voice:   Quality:_____Volume:_____
Clarity:_____Well-trained:_____

_____
Acting ability:_____
Self-projection:_____
Characterization:_____
Self-confidence:_____
Movement:_____
Stage Presence:_____
Carriage:_____

_____
Other description or comments:
```

To the left is a sample of a tryout rating sheet. Naturally, the greater your selection of actors, the more useful this will be.

THE SCRIPT DIRECTOR'S NOTEBOOK

Organization saves time and frustration. When things get hectic and start to fall apart, everyone will feel enough discouragement without adding a lot of unnecessary confusion. The director is the anchor, the North Star, the Rock of Gibraltar. The director must know what he's doing.

A cast and crew must have faith in their director. If they think the man in charge doesn't know what he's doing, they will want to head for the lifeboats before the ship sinks.

How does a director look like he knows all is well when everything is falling around his ears? He prepares and plans early. He works out as many details as possible in advance. He always has an alternate plan. If your first idea doesn't work, be ready with another one.

A director must be everywhere and know everything, but he must not try to do everything himself. A good director asks people to do a job and then trusts them to do it. He should put responsible people in charge of each committee (make-up, costume, lighting, etc.) and then depend on them to do it unless they show they cannot be depended upon. He should not try to take over and do everyone else's job, leaving them feeling very unnecessary.

A good director is open to other people's ideas that may be better than his own. He allows other's creativity to shine and gives credit where credit is due.

A smart director keeps a notebook to help himself get organized and stay organized. No director is such a mastermind he can get along without a notebook in the beginning. Often this notebook gets set aside by the director, after he has memorized the dialogue, so that he can concentrate on motivation, pacing, grouping, etc.

A WORD ABOUT PROMPTERS

Prompters should be eliminated after the first few rehearsals. If the cast knows there is to be a prompter it may cause them to rely on him instead of knowing their lines. It is better to ad lib and cover up flubs than to stop and wait for a prompter to come to the rescue.

A director's notebook should contain the following:
1. A complete version of the play.
2. Diagrams of scenes and plotting.
3. Cues for lighting, music, curtain, and all players directions.
4. List of players and their phone numbers.
5. Rehearsal schedule.
6. Alternate location, if outdoors.
7. Committees, committee heads, and their phone numbers.
8. Schedule of meetings with committees.
9. List of props according to scenes and players.
10. List of furnishings, costumes, and whether they have been borrowed or not.
11. Extra paper for making notes.

Neatness is helpful. Preparing a working notebook in this complete fashion saves production time and preserves the play for another use.

ACTOR'S SIDES

The director provides the actor's scripts. The actor makes his own notebook. On the professional stage the actor's sides consists only of his lines and cues. However, it is a good thing for each actor to have a full copy of the play. Buy copies for all. Copies may not be made if the play is copyrighted. Many actors will memorize the whole play. This is nice when a stand-in is needed. An actor's notebook should contain the following:
1. His lines and cues.
2. His exits and entrances.
3. All his business.
4. Description of his costume.
5. List of all props, according to scene.
6. All directions and changes given him by the director.
7. His own stage markings for pause, stress, etc.

8. Schedule of rehearsal times.
9. Sketch of his make-up and costume.

If possible, attach a sharpened pencil. Valuable rehearsal time shouldn't be wasted hunting pencils. Neatness helps. If an actor can't get to rehearsal, he should make every effort to see that at least his script gets there. If his notebook is what it should be, an understudy can take over.

BLOCKING

One of the director's biggest headaches is positioning actors. Visibility is the first consideration at all times. An audience will not tolerate what it can't see or hear. Think of the center of the stage as the focal point and work outward.

The most obvious problem in grouping and movement is to have people in a position do what they are supposed to do when they are supposed to do it. If Jo is supposed to come downstairs, she better be at the top of the stairs and not at the bottom. If lovers are supposed to kiss, they can't be a mile apart. Yet, grouping should never appear planned but look like a perfectly natural flow of events.

Every stage situation contains movement or motivation for movement. Movement should match the motivation for which it occurs. Nervous Nellies rush around. When we see a snake we jump back. When we are worried, we do not sit down and drift into peaceful sleep. Sick people do not flit around like butterflies. To be convincing, an actor must behave the way people do in real life. When a character's behavior or appearance varies from the norm, the reason must be made obvious.

TYPES OF MOVEMENT

DIRECT — When motives are simple and urgent movements are straight to the point. Because of the need to move about during a dialogue, straight movements are used mostly for exaggerated effect or important movements. Length of movement varies from one and one half steps to a stage "cross." A motive for a direct cross might be, "I have to answer the phone."

Straight, direct movements for straight to the point situations.

Curved line movements for variety of moving and positions.

Broken line movements for going around objects and doing various business.

Sidestepping when in doubt.

Symbolic grouping: A woman is breaking up a married couple. She is placed symbolically between them, "keeping them apart."

INDIRECT — People naturally move in rather curved lines. Unless the motivation is strong, people seldom move in straight lines. This is because we must move around objects or that our attention is leading us off a direct path. A man may walk toward the sofa to sit down, walking around a coffee table to do so. Such curved movements have two advantages onstage. First, they are more graceful than straight lines. And, by moving in varied curves, an actor may end his walk facing any direction he chooses. (Usually it is so that he is facing his audience.) If an actor walks directly to an object and then turns to deliver his line, his movements look inconsistent with his motivation. If he was in such a hurry to get there, he would not stop and turn away when he arrived. Had he been moving in a curved or broken line, he could have ended facing anywhere he chose.

UNCERTAIN — We are either drawn to an object or we are repelled by it. When we are uncertain, we tend to circle it in little arcs rather than in complete circles. Onstage, this is done by taking a step or two sideways. This shows a doubtful state of mind.

GROUPING

Grouping is the arrangement of players in designs which allow them to carry out the plot and be seen by the audience at the same time. Two actors need to be grouped to keep one from covering the other. More than two players must be grouped to prevent chaos.

The puzzle is how to create a world that appears to be going about its everyday business quite naturally while living in a picture frame. On the stage there are no close-ups, no aerial views, no trick photography to rely on. You must make the audience see what you want it to see by unconsciously calling it to their attentions. This is done in several ways — by exaggeration, symbolism, grouping for balance, contrast and emphasis.

COVERING

When a player, action, or object is hidden, it is said to be covered. Amateur players must be trained from the first minute to get out of the habit of covering each other.

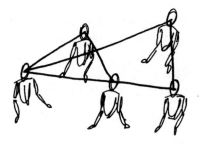

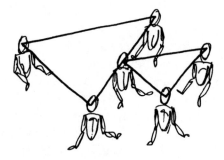

Illustrations above show various ways players can move on stage and still maintain their triangular patterns among themselves.

There are a few instances in which it is desirable to cover something, such as a knife thrust of a murder. Violence should be obscured to hide the fact that it is faked and to soften the effect.

Otherwise, covering is to be avoided. Actors should become adept at keeping themselves uncovered and from covering anyone else.

An indespensible training exercise is to put several players onstage and ask them to move around keeping triangular patterns among themselves. Anytime there are three or more players onstage it should be possible to draw imaginary triangles from face to face. (This is why actors should never bunch up or stand in straight lines.)

An actor who turns more than 90 degrees away from the audience automatically covers his own face. If he talks this way upstage, he must have good motivation for it and compensate by talking louder and clearer. Important dialogue should never be delivered in this obscure fashion.

Covering can also be necessary in special cases such as hysteria, incoherent rage, mob violence, and deliberate mystery.

Talking downstage (keeping the face uncovered) should be arranged naturally by keeping motivation for looking and talking toward the front. If an actor must do his talking to a player upstage, behind him, he can usually solve the problem by glancing at the other person from time to time but saving most of his speaking for delivery toward the audience.

FIGHT SCENES

In love scenes and fight scenes the actions cannot be too violent or too tame. The balance, however, is not easily achieved. Bear in mind the cause for the violence. Is the actor's anger out of proportion to the provocation? Is he really that enraged over nothing? Or shouldn't he be spitting fire over such an insult? Amateurs usually find it hard to work up enough steam or else get carried away with themselves. Anger is one of the easiest emotions to simulate. Break up the fight at the earliest possible moment. Arrange the fight where it is least dangerous for the players

The character nearest the center always carries the most importance.

Balancing a character between two or more figures gives him added emphasis.

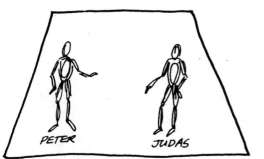

Two characters of equal importance stay across the stage from each other.

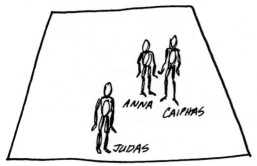

Two characters upstage equals one in the center.

and the set.

Some blows are real. Some are faked. Some are stopped before they are delivered. Deciding which you need to use depends, naturally, upon how likely somebody is to get really hurt. The more violent the blow the more it needs to be faked and covered.

CROWD SCENES

There are several tricks to crowd scenes. Since it is not practical to have a great number of people on-stage, these tricks can be employed to use as few players as possible:

1. Important characters should be in front.
2. If there is a speaker, raise him to another level by having him stand on a chair or another steady object.
3. Have members of the crowd wear bulky clothes.
4. Don't bunch them. Scatter them on different levels.
5. Whenever possible, place some people in entrances so it looks like there are more people outside; have the speaker act as if there were.
6. Don't allow them to stand neatly or move about easily. Crowds normally push and shove. (Just for fun, notice the well-organized crowds running around in Japanese monster movies.) If what you want to do is suggest mob frenzy, create roughness and madness by having someone fall, wear torn clothes, and even knock things over.

Crowds should go about their business by nightfall or whenever the excitement dies. Create the illusion of masses instead of the real thing. When two or three people are gathered together while others are present, the silent should drift away, making their apparent ignorance of what is being said, believable. Soliloquies are always on an isolated stage. Restlessness in crowds and single characters need not be overstressed. Pacing can give way to foot tapping or such.

BUSINESS

Stage business, more than anything else, separates the great from the "not bad." Realistic business can turn a fair play into an outstanding one. Business is anything the actor does onstage.

If an actress, for example, gets up and crosses to the stove to make tea for her guests, her actions serve several functions at once.

1. Her motive for crossing to the stove is revealed.
2. Realism is added.
3. The business of drinking tea is provided for the others.
4. Attention is called to the stove and the dishes.
5. The situation is seen as a friendly gathering.
6. The time of year may be suggested since the tea is hot and not iced.

Eating and drinking is one of the easiest forms of business to provide which is why you see so much of it on television.

THE REASONS FOR BUSINESS ARE MANY

Business is inherent in the script. If the script calls for Judy to shoot Joe, she better have a gun. She may be carrying it; she may find it in the room; she may borrow it from Joe, but she must have a gun. This type of business is required by the play for the plot.

Business is important in the planting of ideas. Sometimes an idea must be planted in the mind of the audience before it is used. If the gun in the shooting scene just happens to be lying on the table when Judy needs it, the audience will rightly suspect it was put there for just that purpose. Guns are not usually lying around like part of the decor. Such obviously contrived business insults the audiences' intelligence. Thus, if a gun is lying on the table, the idea that someone might get hurt by such carelessness should already be planted in the audience's mind.

Business conveys realism. People are always doing something. Only robots and very, very inhibited people and military personnel at attention go around with their arms plastered to their sides —

especially when they are speaking.

Business develops characterizations. Having something to do aids the actor immensely with his characterization. A housewife has endless things to do
around the house. Her work is never done. Even if
she finds time to sit down, she will be sewing, making
out the grocery list, feeding the baby, arranging
flowers, writing letters, etc. If she does not do these
things, women assume she is wealthy enough to have
a maid.

Some typical business should be introduced for each
character early in the play: musicians work with
their instruments, blacksmiths hammer, dancers exercise, etc.

Any movement may emphasize a line. Business
touches before or after an important line give weight
and emphasis to that line. Imagine an actress sewing.
We know she is upset by the way she is stabbing her
needle into the material. Suddenly, she jabs her finger and explodes.

Comic business has to be seen to be appreciated. It
almost defies definition. It is best to study the great
comedians like the Three Stooges, Jerry Lewis, Dick
Van Dyke, the Marx Brothers, etc. Anyone who has
ever seen Harpo Marx in action knows what comic
business is. Harpo never spoke a word onstage. He
didn't have to.

Marx Brothers films are rarely seen anymore but there
are excellent shows on television weekly.

Comic business is anything funny the actor does.
It is the little human touches we imitate from everyday living: it is a little boy chewing a whole package
of gum at once; it is Aunt Lucy stuck to a wad of gum.

REHEARSALS

The object is to get as much accomplished as possible
in the limited time available. Make every minute
count. Nobody has time to waste. If you schedule
a rehearsal from seven o'clock to nine, make sure it
is a rehearsal and not a gossip session.

READ THROUGHS — The first rehearsals should be read-throughs. Gather around a table and read the play, working on expression, voice characterization, emphasis, etc. Interpret the play and analyze the characters. Change lines that cause trouble. All this should be done before memorization. Mistakes are much easier to avoid than to unlearn.

WALK THROUGHS — These initial hours onstage are for blocking in the action. Scripts are read and action (movement and business) noted on the actor's sides. Most people find it easier to memorize an action that is fitted to the lines so that both can be memorized at the same time. Of course, there will be changes up to the end. Fine details can be added later. Too much detail in the walk through confuses actors.

REHEARSING — Scenes are done one at a time until the whole play is memorized. Actors need not come to early rehearsals if they do not appear in the act being rehearsed. Easy scenes are run through without interruption. Difficult scenes are practiced until perfected.

Publish a schedule well in advance so actors and crew can plan ahead. Later rehearsals should go over the whole play every time to establish continuity and aid in memorization. They should be uninterrupted with director's changes and criticisms given afterward. Of course, if something is terribly wrong, it is better to stop and fix it then and there and start all over again.

Allow about five hours from make-up to dismissal. Two dress rehearsals are nice if that is possible. If not, plan the dress rehearsals for two nights ahead of opening night. The dress rehearsal will be tiring and actors need to be fresh. This extra night before opening will give you a chance to fix anything that goes wrong in dress rehearsal. And, there is always something. A regular rehearsal is always nice to keep anybody from forgetting his/her lines.

Never stop or change anything after dress rehearsal begins. Everyone should pretend that it is the real thing and give it his all.

During the first rehearsal, furniture should be in place. The director should have detailed explanations and sketches of the finished set. The set then goes up as soon as it is ready.

Speed rehearsals are when the play is raced through like a film run too fast. Action and words may fumble but no details should be left out. This type of a rehearsal is a great strain but it is worth it. The prompter should be prepared to cut in if the actor misses his cue by a single beat, and the director must call for more speed constantly to keep things zipping along. Nothing else fixes lines so well in the actor's mind. Such speed and concentration help him to forget any self-consciousness. Most importantly, the speedup demonstrates that performance can be done at high speed, so there is no excuse for dragging.

COACHING — Coaching is done with the individual actor to help his acting ability. Amateurs usually need a lot of coaching. This is the reason for the preliminary acting classes. However, a director should spend plenty of time with each individual actor, right down to the smallest walk on. Coaching should not take place during rehearsal time where other actors are kept waiting. Experienced actors can sometimes help to coach inexperienced ones, but only if their advice is not resented.

READY OR NOT, HERE I COME! It should be noted that a play is never ready. You will just have to quit when the time comes and give a performance. There will always be something to improve but there is never enough time.

"BY POPULAR DEMAND"

When a play is really good, it is a shame to give it only once. If possible, schedule another performance soon after your first showing. If it's a smash hit in your own church, perhaps you can take the show on the road to other churches, youth rallies, etc. Better still, invite them to come to you. Get as much mileage out of your hard work, time, and expense as you possibly can.

Every play has hundreds of problems. Never avoid them. Tackle them head on. A problem is a sign that something is wrong. It won't correct itself.

Be careful to solve the big problems first. Beginners have a way of worrying over putting added touches to scenes that are already okay and instead, leave glaring mistakes in other scenes. Make a list of problems and go after them one by one.

The director's function is to solve problems.

Chapter Two: Set Design

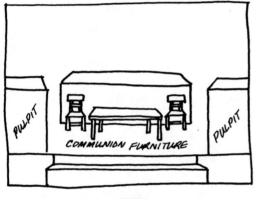

The illustrations above show how a chancel can be transformed to fit the needs for a Christmas play production in which toys learn the true meaning of Christmas. A jack-in-the-box, a teddy bear or robot can appear from behind any of the chancel furniture. An elf can perch on step ladder. The Christmas tree can sit on the organ. Raggedy Ann can sit on step while the ballerina uses the round hassock as a music box. Set-up can be disassembled in only five minutes.

JUST LOOK WHAT YOU CAN DO WITH A CHANCEL

No two church chancels are exactly alike, but they do have plenty in common. Your set designer has much more to work with than you might notice at first glance. Take a long analytical look at the front of your auditorium from the back. Don't compare it with a million dollar theater and complain about what you don't have. Consider all that you do have in the following advantages:

ELEVATIONS — Most chancels are elevated at least eighteen inches. Okay, so you can't play a lot of action on the floor, but at least players can be seen pretty well from the waist up.

LEVELS — The average chancel has more than one elevation, such as a choir loft and steps. Levels are indispensible for variety in grouping and movement.

BACKDROP — Usually a church's front wall is plain, but often the wall houses a baptistry. Some baptistries have painted landscapes that can be incorporated into your scenery. Curtained baptistries can be closed and considered part of the background. Unless you call attention to the baptistry (or other fixtures) it won't conflict with your set at all. People are accustomed to seeing it and won't give it any undue notice.

Nursery or playroom

Courtyard with interior scenes behind.

Classroom

MOVEABLE PULPIT FURNITURE — The rostrum, communion table and chairs, flower stands, and the like can usually be moved to the sides of the auditorium. Naturally, these should be returned to the proper places as soon as possible.

CHOIR LOFTS — Choir lofts can provide extra playing area and additional levels.

MUSICAL INSTRUMENTS — How wonderful to have a piano and organ right on your own stage at all times. Many a secular theater would be envious.

SOUND SYSTEMS — More and more churches are able to afford sound amplification. If it is there, fine, but don't allow your actors to mumble along relying on microphones. Actors should be seen and heard.

LIGHTING — At the least, most churches should be wired so that chancel lights can be turned on while auditorium lights are off. Maybe that's all a director can get, but it's still better than nothing. Then again, there are a few churches that are a director's dream with perfect lighting equipment. Maybe yours is one of those.

ENTRANCES AND EXITS — Little rooms opening onto the stage are fine for entrances, exits, and backstage changes.

Remember, the trick is to work with what you do have. Then you may not have to go out and get a lot of expensive materials.

IMPRESSIONISTIC SCENERY

A setting that occupies only part of the stage is "impressionistic." This is most useful for church theater. It means a designer can put one little setting onstage, or several little settings, separating them by distance and lighting. Changing scenes can be done with a blackout onstage followed by a change of spotlighting.

If distance is suggested between two places, such as a living room and a kitchen, there should not be so much furniture in either place that the two locations seem to be adjoining.

Courtyard with artificial plants and wading pool fountain

Kitchen — Basement — Parlor

Office

The scenery suggests the place and period. Props and furniture are not loaded with a lot of elaborate detail. Instead, the designer relies on "touches" — a few perfect pieces — to set the imagination of the audience to work.

For example, a nursery can be suggested by a crib and a toy or two. If there are props called for by the script, those may be all a clever set designer needs to create his impression. A smart designer will keep impressionistic props and scenery at a bare minimum. Viewers like to use their imaginations.

Plays and skits can be staged anywhere there is room for players to move and an audience to sit. Give your audience credit for plenty of imagination. Let your own directing imagination run wild! A real actor needs only his body and voice — and he can do without the voice!

Wise is the theater group that uses only four folding chairs, a hat rack, and a box of simple props to create an endless parade of scene changes — bus stop, park bench, sofa, office, car, church pew, living room, school, etc.

Chapter Three:
Getting Actors Ready to Act

EXERCISES FOR ACTING SKILLS

Take some time for acting classes prior to rehearsals.
In the long run, this will save you valuable rehearsal
time because beginners often have to be taught how-
to as well as what-to-do. Holding some acting sessions to get everybody over shyness and lack of confidence very early in the game is worth every minute
spent.

There are many exercises for the purpose of helping
young actors get started. Holding classes and working
on these acting techniques before rehearsals begin will
help your crew to get off to a flying start. Nothing is
worse than starting rehearsal with a nervous, self-
conscious cast and a director who doesn't know his
actor's abilities.

The exercises in this chapter are not only beneficial
but packed with fun. Keep the classes light — there
will be lots of mistakes and self-conscious bumbling.
Good. Better now than in rehearsals. Learn to laugh
off mistakes and keep trying. Keep a spirit of experi-
mentation and adventure. Give the actors plenty of
room to stretch their wings and fly.

Actors learn by acting! All the acting experience
they can bring to a part is that much the better for
everyone. These acting classes may be the first
chance some of your cast has had to get their feet
wet. They are learning what they can do and so are

you. Make every session count. You won't regret a minute of it when you come to that first rehearsal.

SELF-CONFIDENCE AND SELF-PROJECTION

Stage fright is both an enemy and a friend. It is an enemy if it inhibits a person from doing his best. A certain amount of stage fright will always be with a good actor. It helps him to do his best by keeping him from getting over-confident. In that way, it is his friend.

The best and only real prevention of extreme stage fright is preparation. Confidence is based on preparation. Preparation is based on practice, practice, practice! Rehearse alone. Know your lines. Develop your own characterization. Make every group rehearsal count, but don't stop there. Polish your performance by working overtime. Your performance will never be better than your preparation. Make this sign and hang it where you must see it every day: **Confidence is built on preparation!**

Self-Projection is a problem for some beginners. Stage presence is another name for the quality that causes some actors to be noticed while others are just "there." Sometimes players with great stage presence are beautiful but beautiful has very little to do with it. The secret lies elsewhere. Self-projection is built on self-confidence. The most attractive players are the ones who forget themselves and play to the audience. They seem to be saying, "I am yours. I am here for your benefit. My performance is my gift to you." This kind of actor gives his very best and the audience loves him for it. Again, self-projection is built on self-confidence and self-confidence is built on preparation.

EXPRESSING EMOTION ONSTAGE

Emotion builds. It starts on a low key and grows until we lose control of it. Building an emotion onstage is done both for the sake of realism and for preparing the audience for what is coming next. One of the most fundamental elements of humor is the unexpected and unless you plan to startle the audience, always build the emotion gradually. For instance, hysterical crying begins with quiet weeping, then turns into sobbing, getting louder until the actor is out of control. (He should appear to be, anyway. Onstage, one really never is.) If an actress suddenly bursts out bawling (one of Lucille Ball's favorite tricks) the audience knows it is strictly for laughs.

Sometimes we are in a situation which demands that our emotions be held in check, but (onstage) the internal struggle must always be visible. For example, if a man's foot goes to sleep in church, his impulse is to get up and stomp, kick, groan. Instead, he mustn't create a scene so he grits his teeth and bears it. But we know he is bearing it by the expression on his face. This is known as disguising emotion.

Before working on the exercises, stress one more thing. Don't be afraid to exaggerate, but don't over exaggerate. Never let your emotion exceed motivation.

The following exercises are designed to teach "shades" of emotion and how they build. Work on each privately and in class. Read aloud in groups of three as separated below and on the following page.

EMOTIONS:
Excitement — Hey, that house is on fire.
Shock — It's my house!
Hysteria — My children are in there!

EMOTIONS:
Gaity — It's a nice morning, isn't it?
Happiness — I like mornings when I can see the sunrise.
Joy — What a glorious day!

EMOTIONS:
Sadness — Today is the anniversary of Mother's death.
Sorrow — My baby is dead.
Heartbreak — My baby is dying.

EMOTIONS:
Annoyance — Your gum popping is driving me crazy!
Anger — Spit out that gum!
Fury — Spit out that gum or I'll break your neck!

EMOTIONS:
Indifference — I don't care.
Distaste — I really don't care.
Contempt — I'm sure I couldn't care less!

EMOTIONS:
Attention — That looks like blood on the floor.
Absorption — It's a trail of blood leading in there . . .
Horror: Oh, no! She's killed herself!

EMOTIONS:
Attention — There's Doctor Allen's car over at Ethyl's house.
Absorption — I wonder if anyone is sick. He's not carrying his bag.
Fascination — Well, I'll be! Ethyl and Doctor Allen are having an affair!

EMOTIONS
Tenderness — Oh, did you hurt your finger, honey?
Compassion — Come and let Mommy kiss it.
Love — Now, now. Mommy's baby will be all right.

EMOTIONS:
Sick — Oh, I don't feel so good.
Sicker — Oh, I feel awful.
Sickest — Oh, I'm sick!

EMOTIONS:
Disinterest — Oh, really.
Doubt — Oh, really?
Total disbelief — Oh, Really!

EMOTIONS:
Dislike — You make me mad.
Disgust — You make me sick.
Hatred — You make me sick!

EMOTIONS:
Uneasiness — I don't think he's coming.
Nervousness — He should have been here hours ago.
Fear — There's a police car. Oh, Lord, it's him.

Now, act the following situations:
Weeping: Pretend your daughter is being married. As the groom slips the ring on her finger you shed a few little tears of joy and sadness.

Panic: Pretend you are a young mother or father. Your baby has pneumonia; he gasps for breath. You are nearly beside yourself with worry. Suddenly he stops breathing.

Fear: You are alone upstairs in bed at night when you hear the front door being pried open. Your apprehension grows as you hear breaking glass. You reach for the phone only to discover that the line is dead.

Anguish: Your only son has been kidnapped. The kidnapper left a note that he would call to discuss the ransom at 8 o'clock. You are in agony worrying until the phone rings at 8 minutes after 8 o'clock.

Desperation: The voice of the kidnapper demands one million dollars for the life of your son. You need time to get that much money. Plead with the kidnapper.

Suffering: On a hike in the woods you fall and hurt your ankle. It is growing dark and you must get back to camp. Wincing with pain, you limp back down the trail. Finally the pain gets to be unbearable.

Agony: While frying chicken, your arm is splattered with hot grease. You are in agony until you get the arm submersed in cold water.

Irritation: You have been shopping all day and your feet hurt. Your husband was supposed to pick you up at 5:00 but he is an hour late, so you must walk home, fuming all the way.

Rage: You arrive home to find your husband on the sofa drinking coffee and watching the ball game. He looks up and says, "Hi, hon, I guess I forgot you."

Some emotions do rise suddenly but don't last long on the same high key.

Joy: You have just received word that your first oil well has hit a gusher.

Embarassment: You doze off in church and are awakened by your own snoring.

Guilt: You are a bank clerk working late one night. The temptations of all that money finally wears down your resistance and you go to the safe, open it, and begin filling your briefcase with money. Suddenly the door opens and your boss walks in.

Laughter: You are working at your desk when you suddenly notice that your secretary has on shoes that don't match.

DISGUISING EMOTION

Sometimes emotions are mixed, like the mother's who cries at her daughters wedding. More often it is a case of feeling one thing and having to show another. This is done by showing one thing with the body and saying another with words. Very often people hide their true feelings behind a brave front or a deceitful smile. To learn the art of saying two things at once an actor must know how to put one emotion into his voice and show another with his body language.

EXERCISES

(Two players) You and your fiancee have not been getting along well lately. Now she is telling you she wants to end the relationship. Her words are stabbing at your heart but you don't want her to know how much you still love her. You turn your back to her and agree with what she says while the pain shows in your face and body.

LAUGHTER AND TEARS — It is difficult to laugh on cue when nothing is funny, yet, to have to do it repeatedly can scare a beginner out of his wits. Agnes Moorehead has a special technique she passes on to beginners. Her advice is to start with a vowel sound.

> O ho ho ho ho ho ho . . . Uh hu hu uh hu . . .
> Ah ha ha ha ha . . .
> Eee hee hee hee, ee hee . . .

CRYING — Crying can be real or fake. Some actors can fake it so well that there is no need to worry about tears because the audience can't usually see them anyway. Movies have to worry about tears but stage actors worry about sounding realistic.

Weeping is a silent, heartbreaking scene. If you have to weep but cannot shed a few tears, fake it by pretending to dry them away. Weeping seems to say that the pain is too great for words, and is very moving. Noisy crying has its use and is fairly easy to fake. The problem is usually the temptation to overdo it. A few sobs go a long way. Hysteria is strong stuff; keep it to a minimum.

SCREAMING — Screaming is a matter of breath control. You need to get a lot of air into the lungs before the cue to scream. Start deep breathing a few breaths before the scream. This builds the emotion and gets you ready for the scream at the same time. Deep breathing shows the audience that your fear or panic is mounting.

Remember, the wilder the actor appears to be, the more in control he really is. Though you may rave and rant and go into convulsions, part of your mind is watching coolly from the sidelines, telling you just what's going on. "Uncontrollability" demands complete control. Practice, practice, practice!

Exercises: Read an emotionally charged play such as *The Crucible* by Arthur Miller or *The Miracle Worker* by William Gibson.

CHARACTERIZATION

"A capacity to transform himself, body and soul, is the prime requirement for an actor." [1]

Building a characterization is the process of bringing a role to life by putting all your physical and mental techniques to work. A printed play can be read and loved, but it was meant to be acted, brought to life by re-creation. The characters wait to be lifted up and have new life breathed into them by an acting troupe.

Building a character begins by thinking as the character thinks. Then the audience discovers how the character looks, how he moves, what he wears and how he wears it, his grooming, posture, and every detail about him. Where does an actor find out these things?

    A. From the play. What the other characters say about his character and from stage directions in the work of some authors.

    B. From history. If the character was a historical figure, research his biographies. If not, read up on the life and times of the period.

    C. From the actor's own rich imagination. What the play or history does not tell you, you are free to invent.

When you are ready to perform a play, have the Biographical Sketch worksheet made up for each player to use and discuss in class. It will benefit the

[1]Stanislavski, *An Actor Prepares*, p.34

actor and director immensely.

Character analysis is the broad view of each character. Usually a little of this information is given by the author, but not always. Often the director and actor work out the rough sketch of a character together. The actor takes over on the fine points. From this rough idea of a character, the real job of characterization can begin. The actor must allow himself to get into the character's skin.

A character analysis list might look like the one that follows from *The Cell*.

Barcus: Young Roman Patrician. Despite his panic to escape, he must show sensitivity and basic goodness which will eventually come to the surface. If not, his character will seem to make too abrupt a change.

Antonius: Young Roman, probably Plebian. Suspicious of the Roman Barcus and contemptuous of the Greek. He is perceptive enough to see his mistakes and Christian enough to change before it is too late.

Inarus: Young Greek. Courageous enough and reckless enough to attack the guard but thrown into panic over the thought of drinking hot lead, as who would not be! His hysteria is understandable so we are sympathetic and applaud his courage in the end. He is the most "picked on" and therefore, the most sympathetic of all. He is also heroic in the end.

Licinia: Young, pretty enough to attract the guards even in her illness. Dying with dignity, she is still more concerned about others than about herself. Must project inner beauty as well as outer.

Joseph: Old enough to have been through most of what life can throw at us. His strength comes from faith that has been tried before. His wisdom comes from knowing (probably from experience) that God delivers in His own way and that way is always right in the end.

Appus: The Patrician friend of Barcus. He is so typically the spoiled, indolent Roman that he cannot begin to comprehend his young friend's decision to die in the arena.

Soldier 1: A typical "hardened to the job" soldier. He obeys orders; asks few questions. Typifies all that made Romans conquerors of the world — Roman pride, prejudice against all other people, love of power and violence.

Soldier 2: A good Roman soldier, but not a typical Army man. This man has sensitivity enough to recognize real courage when he sees it in the Greek. He is able to be touched by kindness and influenced by goodness. He is the kind of Roman who converted into Christianity after coming in contact with other Christians.

SCRIPT PREPARATION

Rehearsing makes the difference between a pro and a ham. For the serious actor, there can never be too much rehearsal.

There is a certain amount of rehearsal and preparation he must do at home. He cannot depend on group rehearsal alone. Some of the things you must do on your own are:

A. Know your lines. Be letter perfect. No one can do it for you.

B. Know your cues. The cues are the last words of the preceding speech or a certain piece of business. Picking up your cues at exactly the right time determines the timing of a scene and is the mark of a pro. Beginners tend to pause between speeches where no pause is motivated.

If you can, memorize the whole play. After enough rehearsal, you probably will anyway. It is good insurance. Never rely on a prompter. Good directors don't use them. Better to ad lib until the line comes back than to wait for some unseen voice to guide you. Better yet, never need prompting!

C. Invent business. Some of your business will be apparent in the script. The director may invent some, but most will be up to you to supply. Some things give you an unlimited supply of business to fill in with.

1. Sewing. Keep a mending box handy so a woman can always have something to do when she sits down. Needlework is

a never-ending job.

2. Writing. Keep a diary. Write letters. Write memos. Do homework. Copy recipes. Pay bills.

3. Cleaning. Housework is never done whether inside or outside. There's always something to clean, straighten, or repair.

4. Eating and drinking. The old standby. Don't rely on it too heavily, however. Try for something more imaginative.

When it comes to inventing business, use imagination and detail. The director may tell you to sew, but it is up to you to add the little touches like threading the needle, looking for thread, ripping out, etc. Details add color and realism.

D. Write your own "Silent Script." Silent script is what the character is thinking when he is not talking. It is the secret of good reaction. The silent script keeps an actor from standing around with a blank look on his face waiting for his next speech.

Sample of silent script or unwritten dialogue below is in italics.

Doorbell rings.

Mary: *Oh dear, who can that be? I'll never get through if this keeps up.*

Doorbell rings.

Joe: Hello, my name is Joe Hardy. May I have a moment of your time?

Mary: *Egad! A door-to-door salesman!*

Mary: Well, I am terribly busy.

Joe: Oh, I promise not to take up more than five minutes to show you something that could change your life.

Mary: *Probably a can opener. I'm gonna hate myself for this.*

ACTOR'S SIDES

On the professional stage the actor's sides consist only of his lines and his cue phrases. However, it is a good thing to have a full copy of the play, and just as simple for the church production staff to make full copies for all. Many actors will memorize the whole play. This is nice in an emergency when a

∩   Chair

∧   Sofa

ρ   Breath

•   Small Pause

σ   Large Pause

↦   Direction for actor to face

ᖸ   Downstage turn

⸾   Upstage turn

←--- Backward steps

stand-in is needed. An actor's notebook should contain the following:

1. His lines and cues.
2. His exits and entrances.
3. All his business. (Any action he does on stage.)
4. Description of his costume.
5. List of all props, according to scene.
6. All directions and changes given him by the director.
7. His own stage markings for pause and stress, etc.
8. List of rehearsal times.
9. A sketch of his make-up and costumes.
10. His silent script.

If possible, attach a spare sharpened pencil to the notebook. Valuable rehearsal time must not be wasted on sharpening pencils. Keep the record as neat as possible. Should the actor be unable to get to a rehearsal or the performance, he must make every effort to see that his script gets there. If his notebook is what it should be, an understudy can take over with much less frustration.

MEMORIZING

Real rehearsal cannot begin until you know your lines. These are some tips to make the job of memorizing a little easier. As soon as you get your script, read it over many times to fix it in your mind. Walk through the scenes, learning association. Practice moving about and doing little bits of business synchronizing movement with words. Some actors find it helpful to memorize the whole play, as well as their own part. If you can do that, good. Repeated rehearsal is an aid to memorization. To make sure you know your lines, ask someone to read your cues and recite them back.

Earmarks of a careless actor:

1. Slow on cues.
2. Never sure of his lines.
3. Speaks without punctuation. Expressionless.
4. Drops out of character when speaking.
5. Fidgets. Makes unnecessary movements.
6. Fails to speak audibly. Drops last word.
7. Is late.
8. Does not cooperate with the whole cast to

project the play rather than himself.

The following is a list of Ten Commandments for Actors and is suggested as a guide for dealing with some foreseeable problems.

1. Thou shalt not look at the door if someone fails to enter on cue.
2. Thou shalt not look if someone makes an unrehearsed noise.
3. Thou shalt not look at the floor unless thou art speaking about the floor, for verily, the audience will think thou art looking for thy lines.
4. Thou shalt not look at the prompter for thy lines. Find an excuse to go off stage and get thy line, then carry on as though nothing were wrong.
5. Thou shalt not look at friends in the audience.
6. Thou shalt not start over if thee blow thy lines. Ad lib. Pretend to know what thou art doing and bluff until thou dost know.
7. Thou shalt not walk in a straight line onstage unless thou hast a reason.
8. Thou shalt not bunch, but always keep thy triangles and never cover thy fellow actor.
9. Thou shalt not covet the major roles, but shall strive to make thine own role an outstanding creation.
10. Thou shalt never do anything onstage unless thou hast a reason. Even if thou art doing nothing, thou shalt know the reason why.

INTERPRETING SCENES: THE BEST EXERCISE

The best overall exercise for an actor is reading plays. Assign parts to students and have them read before the class after about fifteen minutes preparation. Switch parts around so everyone can do a variety of roles.

If you have time for nothing else, at least do this. It gives the beginner invaluable experience in a multitude of theater problems in the least amount of time.

To obtain scenes at no cost, go to the public library. You can find the most popular plays in more than one anthology so you can have more than one copy of a play.

If you aren't so lucky at the library, these are
some of the wonderful paperbacks for students:

Scenes for Young Actors
edited by Lorraine Cohen (Avon, 1973)

Fifty Scenes for Student Actors
edited by Lewy Olfson (Bantam Books, New York,
1970)

PANTOMIME

Pantomime is a wordless play. To appreciate what
pantomime really is, you must watch the masters
such as Harpo Marx, Dick Van Dyke, Sid Caesar,
Jerry Lewis, Red Skelton, and, of course, the great
Marcel Marceau.

Guidelines for Pantomime:
1. Thought always precedes action. First, the
   look, then the thought, then the action. We
   see the candy; we want the candy; we take
   the candy. See. React. Respond.
2. Facial expression usually precedes body action.
3. Exaggerate movement and expression so it
   will be clearly understood by the little old
   lady in the back. Make action big, broad,
   and definite.
4. Use upstage arm whenever possible to avoid
   covering face.
5. All movement must be clearly motivated. We
   see the candy. We lick our lips in anticipation,
   We pick up the candy and unwrap it, crush the
   wrapper and throw it away. (The wrapper
   tells the audience we are eating candy and
   not a banana.)
6. Visualize your character in minute detail.
   Know who you are, how you feel, and what
   you want to do before you try to show others.
7. Visualize your stage in minute detail before
   you begin. Know location of furniture, props,
   other characters, etc. If you do not see them
   in your mind, no one else will by your actions.
8. Rehearse to perfection.

Exercises:
Pantomime a short (3-5 minute) scene such as:
Birdwatcher feeding birds in winter

Bored child in grown-up movie
Writer with writer's block
Artist painting wiggly model
Dog catcher
Rescuing cat stranded in tall tree

IMPROVISATIONS: THE OLYMPICS OF ACTING EXERCISES

An improvisation is a play in which actors make up their own scripts as they perform. There are two versions of the same idea. An improvisation may be performed on the spot, extemporaneously; or it may be performed after it has been built into a more finished product before it is seen by an audience. Either way it is a director's dream. Why?

Improvised plays require almost no advance preparation. They do not cost one inflated dime. It gives actors a chance to express themselves while they are learning acting technique. It is creative, challenging, and fun. For the amount of time he has, the improvised play gives the drama teacher/director the most for his money. Some of the things the improvising actor learns are:
- To ad lib under pressure.
- To be aware of audience reaction at all times.
- To give and take stage.
- The importance of interdependence with other actors (ensemble acting).
- To develop all his senses, physical and mental.
- To direct himself.

It is rather like throwing a non-swimmer into the water and telling him to sink or swim.

There are a few simple rules to remember in group improvisations:
1. Say something even if it is not brilliant. This will give the other person something to go on while you think of something that is brilliant. Usually whatever is on the top of your head is good enough.
2. Don't filibuster. Keep your speeches short. Nothing is more boring than one person monopolizing a show.
3. Don't use all your ammunition in one speech. In a fight you might say, "I hate you. You're

mean to the kids. You make fun of my
mother, and I want a divorce." If you do,
you've used up topics for four conversations.

4. Let your natural storytelling instinct carry
   you along and tell you how to build a climax
   and when to end.
5. Use whatever hand props and furniture you
   need but no more than necessary. Concentrate
   on acting, not staging.

Now that you know how to begin, you need a
situation. The idea is to set up two or more characters in opposition to each other. Pick opposite
types and put them both in a situation they feel
strongly about, then watch them explode. For example: arch conservative father versus hippie son,
or brainy older brother tries to help kid brother who
is flunking math.

The possibilities are endless. Just remember that
drama, by definition, is conflict. The problem is
where the action is. The solution is the climax or
the anti-climax. Two persons agreeing is not good
drama. Where there is no conflict, there is no in-
terest.

Notice what people argue about. Keep a list of pet
peeves and common hates. Ask yourself what makes
people fighting mad. If you observe people and
keep a handy list, you can get an improvisation
going on a moment's notice. Other ideas come from
newspapers, movies, story plots, and television.

When do you stop an improvised play?
1. Before it dies. Quit while you're ahead.
2. When you have made your point.
3. When the sketch isn't going anywhere. Some
   situations will never really get off the ground
   because there is nowhere for them to go. Or,
   and this is more likely the case, those partic-
   ular actors are just not suited for that situation. In a stalemate neither side is getting
   anywhere. The actors begin to repeat themselves. The only thing to do then is for one
   of the actors to stomp off in a rage or for the
   director to stop the skit.

In any case, an improvisation should not run past
five minutes unless the audience is positively

COSTUME INFORMATION

Play: _William Tyndale_
Period: _Henry VIII   C-1550_
Actor: _Todd_
Character: _Edward_
Sizes: _14 - boys_
Sleeve Length:_____
Neck:_____
Blouse or shirt: _14_
Skirt: (length)_____
Pants inseam:_____
Shoes: _size 2 - slippers_
Dress Size:_____
Coat Size:_____
Hat size or head measurement:_____
Glove size:_____
Costumes needed — _Vest with puff sleeves,_
Act I: _shorts._

Act II:

Act III:

Sketches:

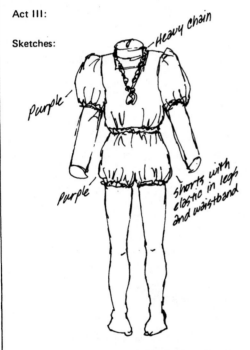

Heavy chain

purple

purple

shorts with elastic in legs and waistband

Notes for Costumer: _Needs leotards. For blouse underneath wear yellow shirt backwards. Borrow yellow leotards from Ann. Make top from girls' pattern._

spellbound. (It will be sometimes.)

SPONTANEITY

Spontaneity is the key word in improvisations, so don't try to work out too much of the plot before the actors begin. Let it go where it will. However, after a play has been built by improvising, it may be in need of some polishing before it can be performed for the church. What is experimental in class needs to be perfected for the general audience. You may lose a little freshness this way, but no two performances are ever exactly alike. There is still plenty of room for spontaneity.

You will find some actors have an outstanding gift for improvising. Let these actors carry the load while the shyer players fill the supporting roles. Don't let anyone think he can't participate because he is not good at it. Every comedian needs a straight man and every lead role must have supporting roles. Besides, every actor gets better with practice and that's the whole idea.

SOME IDEAS FOR IMPROVISATION:

— A conservative father and his long-suffering wife greet their son coming home from a year at college. They are shocked by his long hair and beard and hip girl friend.
— Mother and daughter shop for clothes. Mother wants daughter to buy with a taste for fashion. Daughter wants the mod look.
— Two junior boys disrupt a Sunday school class.
— A Christian calls on a friend in jail. There he meets an alcoholic.
— A church worker calls on two or three elderly ladies seeking help for the church social. They turn her down with lame excuses. One is a hypochondriac, one is slightly deaf, one is a social swinger in the Golden Age set. Finally, she calls on a teenager who is more than willing to help.
— A group of teens call on a factory owner to talk over the possible ways to help prevent pollution by his factory.
— A father with an alcohol problem tries to discourage his son from taking drugs.
— A songbook and a pew talk about attendance problems.

Chapter Four:
Costumes and Props

BUILDING A COSTUME DEPARTMENT OUT OF POVERTY

You can go all out for costumes without going bankrupt if you learn a few simple tricks about how to make old things into new.

Remember, costumes are seen from a distance so they don't have to be perfectly stitched and every thread does not have to match. Of course, if you have the time and can go to a great expense, you will want your creation to hold up for a long time.

Take the time to make a work of art, if you so desire. Yet, for a one shot deal on a shoestring, make do with what you can put together in a hurry. Don't let the fear of "too much trouble" hold up your ambitious plans.

Hints and illustrations in this chapter are designed to help you start with plain material and clothes from yard sales, attics, and hand-me-downs.

If you are doing many costumes and have several individuals helping, a form like the one on the left will be helpful. This will give the wardrobe workers a wealth of information they can use and pin to the costumes to help keep track of what is what.

Things you need are lying around the house right now. If you put this list where the ladies of the church can see it, and make an appeal, they will help you find all that you need and more. A good

Basic Sack Dress

Coat-Look

Sashed & Shortened

With Sleeves and Trim

Angel Sleeves

Two Basic Robes

costume mistress is an avid junk collector. Often, what looks like junk to others looks like a costume or prop to her.

Costume treasures include:

Old jewelry — bangle bracelets, pendants, earrings, chains, dinner rings, etc. Plastic can't be used for Bible plays but is rather for modern theatrics. Rope, braid, fringe, and trims of all kinds are helpful. Trims change with the period. Lace does not belong on Bible costumes. Research!

Old hats — especially pillboxes. Hats can be restyled by changing brims and trims. Pillboxes can be the base in making turbans and other head coverings.

Sandals — all types. Period shoe styles.

Safety pins and straight pins. Threads and needles. Scissors.

Blankets and sheets — in solids and stripes.

Baskets — all shapes and sizes.

Pottery — Anything Mediterranean looking.

Materials — remnants. Scarves.

Bags and pouches, women's purses.

Make-up.

BIBLE COSTUMES: VARIATIONS OF THE BASIC SACK DRESS

Bible plays are the easiest period to costume — if you know what to do with a few basics. The basic robe for men or women (and children) is the fundamental "sack dress." (It is named for the venerable gunny sack, undoubtedly. Incidentally, this material makes a dandy beggar's robe.) The "dress" is three or four yards of anything except obviously modern synthetic material folded in half crosswise, seamed up both sides about three-fourths of the way. The other one-fourth should be left for armholes. A roomy neckline is cut in one end or the other. The bottom end is hemmed or left to fringe. That, in four easy steps, is it! You can quit right there or go on to fancier things.

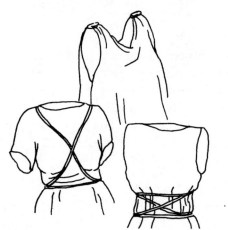

Greek and Roman fashion variations for upper class members: a wide and flowing dress, pinned at shoulders with large broaches; a dress with little sleeves and cords wrapped over the shoulder; and, a midriff wrapped with slender cords.

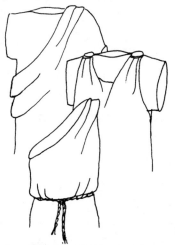

Three versions of Greek and Roman menswear: a one-sleeved version of robe over slender, short-sleeved version in contrasting colors; a basic sack dress over tunic; and, an off-the-shoulder version like that of a Greek toga.

Two versions of Medieval costumes, above. Basic garment attached only at shoulders and worn over another basic garment and sweater and, on the right, a basic costume with a man's shirt worn backwards underneath. Another version of the basic costume is placed over. The rop on top is gathered and sewed together at the shoulders. The two front side panels are double the width of the back.

WHAT THE WELL-DRESSED SHEPHERD IS WEARING

For centuries the shepherds in annual Christmas pageants have worn boy's or men's bathrobes. Not a bad idea, but a dead giveaway that your costume department is on a tight budget. Ban the bathrobe? No, no, don't be hasty. All that good material shouldn't go to waste. Disguise it, instead.

Pretend the robe is a basic sack dress. Then belt it (with hemp rope, maybe); tuck its modern collar out of sight; wrap it tightly (with a wide sash, possibly); and/or add a rough blanket cape over it. The idea is to get rid of the "new" look. Make it look like a Jewish peasant instead of an American father.

You can do the same sort of thing with ladies dresses — just be sure that the material does not look like it obviously came from a modern, 20th century department store.

GREEK AND ROMAN HIGH FASHION

The Greek and Roman looks are also easy with variations of the basic sack dress. When costuming upper class Greeks and Roman, use lighter fabrics in white and pastel colors for a more opulent look than that of the homespun peasant clothes.

Remember, you are not trying to duplicate the exact garment worn by the ancients. Your costume will be a modified version of the original. Yet, with the right touches, your simple costumes can look sensational. Nothing helps a play more than great looking costumes. Take heart in the fact that theater has no close-ups. Your costumes have to look good from a distance, which gives you a lot of room to play. The costume that looks marvelous from the front row doesn't have to be able to stand close inspection.

THE MEDIEVAL LOOK

The Medieval costumes are similar to Bible costumes in their use of loose, flowing garments. The Medieval period is distinctive for its abundant use of beautiful materials — woolens, brocades, etc.

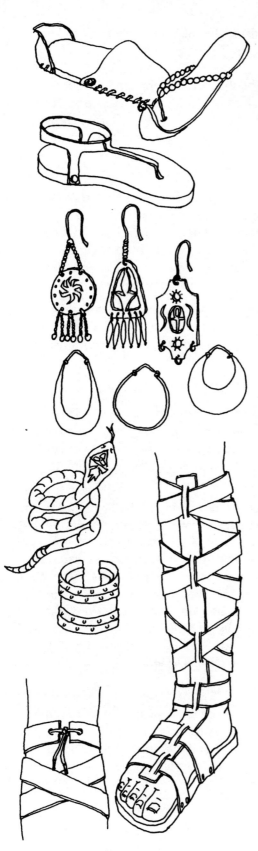

SANDALS

Sandal styles have not changed much throughout the centuries. The natural straw styles of today are perfect for Bible plays. Even wedge heels are all right for royal women. The illustrations show the variety of Mediterranean footwear. The only thing that won't pass is plastic, rubber, or sandals that look like recent inventions.

Sandals can be adorned with jewelry for the well-dressed royalty and upper-class members.

JEWELRY

Earrings were worn in pierced ears by both men and women. They could not be too large or too ornate. They were made of silver, gold or enamelled. Nothing that looks plastic should be worn. In ancient times, only the wealthy could afford earrings and often times they hung down to their shoulders.

Rings for the nose were similar to the loop earrings in the illustrations.

Rings for the fingers were popular and worn on every finger.

BRACELETS

Mediterranean people were fond of all kinds of brace-lets. Like they did, you can also wear several at a time on both arms. Ankle bracelets, too, are perfectly ac-ceptable.

The styles of today are about the same as styles of bracelets in Bible times. Costume jewelry that can't be worn one way can be taken apart and re-fashioned into something that can be. The gaudy, clunky pieces you wouldn't be caught dead in offstage usually look great onstage. Remember, a wise costume mistress never throws anything away.

ROMAN SANDALS

You may experiment and come up with an easier way to make a Roman sandal, but this is one of the more simple ways known to the author. Lace narrow strips of imitation leather through slits in a wider piece that fits from ankle to knee. The upper lacings need not be attached to the sandal itself. You can wear an ordinary men's sandal and wear the lacing

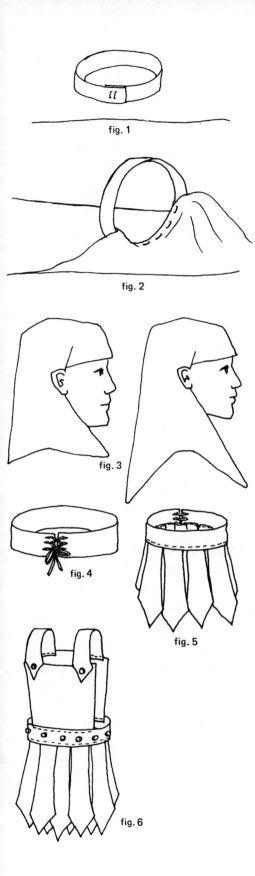

fig. 1

fig. 2

fig. 3

fig. 4

fig. 5

fig. 6

above it. Onstage it will look authentic enough. At a distance it should be difficult to tell if it is attached or not.

The strips can be tied by tying dark shoestrings to a slit in the end of the lacing strips.

EGYPTIAN HEADDRESS

Cut a cardboard band (poster board or slightly thicker) about two inches wide to fit the head. Form a circle and staple securely. (See fig. 1)

Lay the circle on a rectangle of thin material about 1¼ to 1½ yards long, 36 inches wide. Exact size depends on the wearer.

Staple the side of one edge to the underside of the cardboard circle. Staple it about halfway around or a little less. (See fig. 2)

Bring up the material, over the circle band, and over the crown of the head.

Tuck the side edges behind ears. Length should be slightly below shoulders. (See fig. 3)

Follow the same procedure for Egyptian women, using a large square of material instead of a rectangle. Her version should be longer, too.

ROMAN SOLDIER

Cut a strip of imitation leather to fit the waist. Tie in back with shoestrings through slits in ends. (See fig. 4)

Cut pointed strips about 16 inches long (from waist to just above the knee). Sew strips to waistband. (See fig. 5)

Cut leather (imitation) vest piece (called a breastplate) to cover chest and another for back. Sew to top of waistband. (See fig. 6)

Sew strips of imitation leather (pointed at one end) to the back piece at the top. Bring these pieces over the shoulders to form straps. Fasten in front with heavy brads. (See fig. 6)

Attach gold brads to look like nail heads around the waistband.

Wear over knee length red tunic. Add a red cape and Roman sandals.

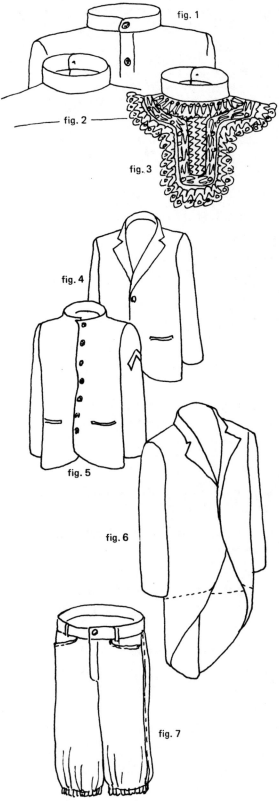

fig. 1

fig. 2

fig. 3

fig. 4

fig. 5

fig. 6

fig. 7

PERIOD COSTUMES FROM THE RUMMAGE

Costumes for early periods naturally require some work. Face it. It can't be helped. Still, the rewards are so worthwhile!

There are so many stories from church history just begging to be dramatized. Don't be frightened off by the prospect of making elaborate costumes. You may already have a lot more to work with than you realize. The secret, as usual, is to start with what you have before you worry about what you don't have.

For example, consider a few things a good costumer can do with a man's old white shirt.

In the '50s it was the shirt for dress. There should still be loads of them around.

Cut off the collar and you have a tunic neck, worn with most military uniforms of the past. (See fig. 1)

Wear it backwards and you have a turtleneck — or a priest's collar. (See fig. 2)

Wear it backwards and add lace to collar and cuffs for the 17th and 18th century dandy. (See fig. 3)

See what can be done with a man's solid suit jacket. Where do you find them? Anywhere there is used clothing.

Turn up the lapels and add extra buttons and felt insignias to make military coats. (See figs. 4 & 5)

Add matching material to the back for nineteenth century frock coats with "tails." (See fig. 6)

Ordinarily, solid color, woolen trousers can do for most men's costumes. You may need to sew stripes up the outside seam or take off cuffs or make some other slight alterations. Once you have found the right color and material, your problems are pretty well solved in the trouser department. Any non-shiny material can be substituted if it doesn't look synthetic. Shorten and add elastic at the knee for knickers. (See fig. 7)

You probably thought men's costumes would be most difficult. Now that you've seen what can be done with all that stuff in the attic, perhaps you

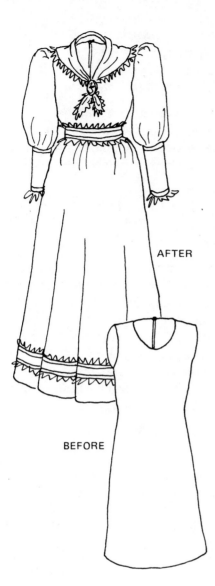

AFTER

BEFORE

have changed your mind.

LADIES FASHIONS

Ladies fashions have a way of repeating themselves. The billowing formals of the 1950's are reminscent of the ball gowns of the 1850's. Today's "romantic" look is drawn from the Romantic periods of history. This makes your costuming job a lot easier.

Start by looking through the history books and art books for portraits of the period you need. Note the styles and materials. Notice any similarity between styles of that period and what girls have been wearing in the last few years.

Go through all the used clothing in your storage places and everyone else's. Then tackle the thrift shops, Goodwill stores, yard sales, etc. You are bound to find a lot of things you can alter to suit your purposes.

You can add all sorts of things to a plain dress: sleeves, full skirts, sashes, ruffles and trims.

PROPS

The "prop man" or "stage manager" is responsible for all properties — anything used onstage.

There are two or three types: hand props (anything handled by the actor), scenery props (anything used to dress the stage such as curtains, rugs, pictures, vases, flowers, books and bookshelves, etc.), and sometimes, special effects.

Special visual effects can be the prop man's job if for no other reason than because he's the only one there to do it. Effects such as smoke, snow, fire, blood, rain on umbrellas, and all other such myriad little details have to be done by someone. If you can't have one person covering just these duties, the prop man will have to cover it.

A director will naturally work closely with his prop man. This should make both very happy because the job requires boundless imagination, and one person never has enough.

Actors can't rehearse long without hand props, so the sooner these are ready, the better. The prop man will want to begin planning and collecting as soon as he gets his script.

The first thing a prop man does is read the script and make a list, scene by scene, of all the props that will be needed. Then he should go over every detail with the director for changes and additions.

The second thing to do is start digging around in everybody's junk for the things needed. Other's throw-aways may be a prop man's treasures.

Begin plans for everything you can beg, borrow, buy, or build, even rent. It is never too soon to start collecting. Borrowing should be kept at a rock bottom minimum because it is too difficult to replace broken valuables. Rental shops are wonderful allies, but don't count on them having what you need at the last minute. Building, of course, takes time. Flea markets are your second best friend; Aunt Nancy's attic is your first.

BIBLE PROPERTIES — ANYTHING USED BY ACTORS

To know what Bible play actors should use onstage, we have to know how Bible people lived. There is not a lot of variation over the years covered by the several hundred years of the Bible, but a few changes are worth pointing out. To be really accurate, actors should research the period they are portraying. Briefly, two periods are most useful to Bible actors: The Mosaic Period and the Time of Christ.

Until the death of Moses, the Hebrews had been a nomadic tribe, living in tents, moving when it became necessary to find food for their animals. Upon settling in Canaan, their homes took the more permanent forms of mud cement or limestone. They had learned much from their stay in Egyptian sophistication. Livestock in Canaan was mostly sheep, so cloth was mainly wool or skin from goats. Skins were scraped for belts, ropes, sandals, and wine bags. Baking was done in outdoor oven-like little mounds. Sweeping was done with thorn brooms. While the garbage from villages was thrown into the streets for dogs, the Hebrews were not really a dirty type of people. Hands and feet were washed as a matter of courtesy for visitors who came in from the dusty roads. Wash basins and water jugs were kept filled by the front door for everyone's comfort and convenience.

Families tried to be self-sufficient, but trading was common when caravans of merchants crossed their paths. Life was simple, easy-going, and even dull. The men tried to compensate with stories and music.

DISHES

Earthenware of any shape or size, crude and rough, was used in poorer homes. Dishes in the wealthier homes were sometimes embellished with gold overlay. Pottery in primitive styles can be purchased, still, in ten-cent stores or roadside novelty stores. Imperfects and chipped pieces can sometimes be purchased at a fraction of cost. Just one of those enormous, colorful water jars (2 or 3 feet high) does wonders for an ancient setting.

Wooden bowls, too, make excellent props. For dippers, gourds are just the thing.

FURNITURE

Regular tables with sawed off legs are good. Seats can be orange crates covered with blankets. Brick design can be painted on boxes for ovens or storage.

Beds may be made of blankets, pallets. Cushions add a nice touch. Nomads carry their beds on their backs and you should, too. When a night comes, they did, and do, roll up in a shawl under the stars.

SCROLLS

Scrolls were carried in cylindrical pouches made of fine leather. Several scrolls could be conveniently carried in one pouch attached to a scribe's belt. Valuable scrolls were stored in earthenware jars and sealed with wax. The Dead Sea Scrolls were found preserved in this manner.

There are several ways to make scrolls from the simplest plain round broom handle cut to desired

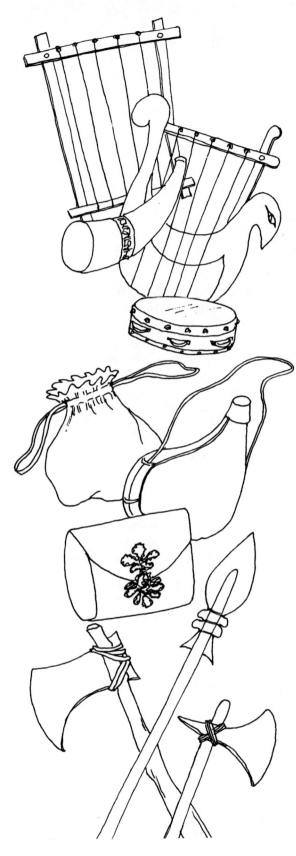

length and wrapped with paper to fancy ones made with carved wooden dowels and something that looks like skins. The idea is to staple, tape, or glue paper to sticks. Roll the left side to the right so that when it is unrolled it will read from right to left, as the Hebrews read.

MUSICAL INSTRUMENTS

Rams' horns are still around as the prized possession of hunting dog owners. Sometimes they can be found in sporting good stores. If you think finding one is trouble, wait until you try to blow one. Still, they are worth all the trouble to a Bible play.

Harps should be plywood, painted, and strung with cord. They don't sound very well but they look pretty.

POUCHES

Make a variety of pouches for waterskins, money-belts, seed and feed bags.

Sew three sides of a rectangle and pull drawstrings through the hem in the open end. Burlap is best.

The new fake furs are great, too, such as suede-cloth.

Many ladies handbags can be used just the way they are if they have no plastic or modern materials to date them. Check the rummage first before you spend money. The types of bags shown here are made from scraps.

TOOLS AND WEAPONS

Find an old broom, mop handles, or smooth tree branches that fit comfortably in the hand. Cut to desired length. Saw a split in one end as if you were sawing the wood in two lengthwise. From very thin plywood or heavy cardboard, cut the shape of axes, spears, etc. Insert "blades" into splits in handles. Glue and/or tie into place, as is indicated in the illustration. Spray "blades" silver or metallic to look real.

Of course they won't look real. The best option is to get a modern tool and disguise it to look old.

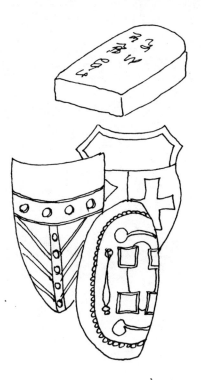

TABLETS OF STONE

Styrofoam sheets are wonderful for a prop department. Shapes can be drawn on the surface and cut out with a Styrofoam cutter (a hot wire apparatus). Florists usually have them and will cut simple designs for you. (Offer to pay for this service. However, the florist may do it without charge.) Styrofoam can be sprayed any color with florist spray. Many Hollywood props such as stones and boulders that fall on people are made of Styrofoam.

SHIELDS

Lightweight boards are best for shield material. Cut them to desired shape. Attach handles in back with old drawer pulls or leather straps using screws and bolts. Paint them silver or brown. If boards are not available, there is always good old cardboard as a possible building material!

Chapter Five: Make-up

A LITTLE GOES A LONG WAY

Church play make-up need not be a headache or
cost a fortune. Except for special effects, you
need only enough to emphasize an individual's
features and keep them from being invisible to
the person in the back row.

These are some of the reasons everyday cosmetics
are preferable to grease paint:
1. Amateurs do a much better job with it.
2. It is easier to put on and take off.
3. It costs less. Some of the least expensive
   brands are better than the high priced.

4. Because churches are not so big or so
   elaborately lighted as a stage, grease paint
   is not needed.
5. Everyday cosmetics are easier to acquire.
   Grease paint has to be ordered if you don't
   have access to a store that carries it, and
   very few do.

Hold a class session or two to teach your actors
how to do their own make-up well in advance of
rehearsals.

Ask ladies to clean out their make-up boxes and
give you what they don't want. You probably
won't have to buy a thing. Two articles are
absolutely indispensible — dark eyebrow pencil

and red lipstick. With these two essentials, almost anything can be accomplished. Wrinkles, freckles, wounds, scars, sunburn, measles, beauty marks, age spot, mustaches, sideburns, and sores can all be made. Also, eyes can be lined, teeth blacked out, and rouge applied, not to mention painting eyebrows and lips.

Materails to collect:

Make a list and put it where the ladies can all see it so that they will know exactly what you need. The church bulletin is one place where you might advertise for the items you need.

1. Eyebrow pencils — black, brown, gray.
2. Lipsticks in all colors. If you do have to buy some, the cheap ones are fine.
3. Eyeshadow in all colors, especially white.
4. Tissue. Inexpensive sorts will do.
5. Foundation in all shades. Liquid, cream, or pancake.
6. Rouge — liquid or powder.
7. Lip brushes and liner.
8. Powder — light and dark shades, compact or loose.
9. Black mascara.
10. Cotton balls, powder puffs, cotton swabs.
11. Mirrors, tweezers, scissors.
12. Cold cream, cleansing cream, soap.
13. Make-up capes or rags to keep make-up off clothes.
14. Shoe boxes and plastic bags for storage.
15. Wigs — all colors and kinds.

PRINCIPLES OF MAKE-UP APPLICATION

Exaggerate in proportion to the distance from which you will be viewed. Distance and bright lights blur features. You won't have to paint up for the average church the way you would for Madison Square Garden, however! Experiment under the lighting you will be using in performance. You can't see yourself onstage the way the audience will. The director, however, should take on the critical eyes and perspective of the audience as he looks at his cast.

Avoid the temptation to flatter yourself with make-up. Your aim is to adapt your face to the character's face. If your character is plain and homely go ahead and make yourself plain and homely. Good characterization depends on it. If your character is pretty, naturally you must make her as gorgeous as possible. Just remember, a real pro is not afraid to look ugly for a role.

Dirty, poorly applied make-up distracts. Avoid obvious, garish make-up unless the characterization demands it. If the characterization demands it, anything goes.

TECHNIQUES FOR THE NATURAL LOOK

EYES — Darken brows with pencil. For the natural look, avoid bright colored shadow and use only white to bring out the sparkle and contrast. White shadow, darkened brows, a touch of mascara and beige lipstick are usually enough for men.

LIPS — Lipstick is nicest in pink and beige. Red is best for period styles and special effects. Lip gloss is good, too. Men may object at first to wearing any lipstick, but they need to realize that it serves another purpose besides helping the lips to be seen. Lipstick or gloss helps keep the lips moist. An actor has enough to worry about without suffering dry, cracked lips when he's trying to speak.

FOUNDATION — Shine and gleamer are good for the fresh scrubbed look and a glowing face looks pretty under stage lights.

For darker skin tones, use a few drops of very dark foundation blended in the palm with white hand lotion. After this mixture is blended in one hand, apply with both hands on all the skin that shows when the costume is worn, right down to the toes, if necessary. This gives a smooth, golden brown skin tone and saves a fortune on expensive dark foundation.

MAKE-UP FOR CHILDREN

Children must always have the natural look. The only exceptions may be when one is doing comedy or special effects. The natural look does not mean,

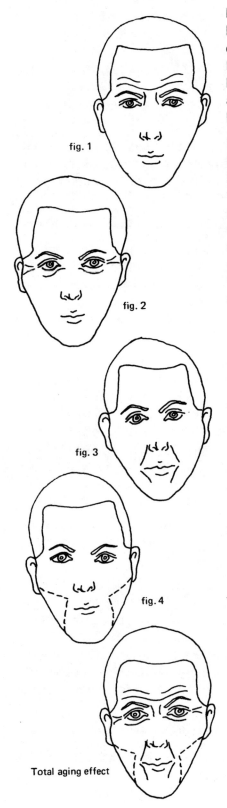

fig. 1

fig. 2

fig. 3

fig. 4

Total aging effect

however, that they should have no make-up, but rather that their make-up should not be obvious. And oh, how they love to wear it! It makes them feel so adult and helps them do a better job of characterization. They really do need a little to accent their delicate features under the bright lights.

Begin by stroking some color on their brows with brown pencil. Shadow the eyelids with light green, blues, pastel brown or white. Carefully paint the tips of eyelashes with mascara. Eyeliner should not be necessary unless your lights are very bright and your audience is far away. Avoid any harshness of effect. Foundation can be eliminated except for the cheeks where a little rouge or blush will bring out their natural rosiness. Lipsticks should be beige and pink.

Hairstyles must be natural. Short or long, all it needs is to be clean and shiny. Elaborate coiffeurs are out of place on little girls. If you're doing a period play, do a little research into the hairstyles of the day, remembering that children's hairstyles have changed very little throughout the ages.

SPECIAL EFFECTS — AGING

Frown lines — Frown. Fill in natural lines with sharp brown or gray pencil. (See fig. 1)

Laugh lines — Smile. Pencil lightly with eyebrow pencil two or three of the tiny lines that appear at the corners. (See fig. 2)

Circles — Faint circles under the eyes show illness or age, and fatigue. These are made by smudging a little gray or brown shadow in a semicircle under the eye. (See fig. 2)

Mouth lines — Smile. Draw lines in the creases from nose to chin. (See fig. 3)

Hollow cheeks — Suck cheeks in. Lightly fill in hollows with gray or brown shadow. Blend smoothly until no "edges" can be detected. (See fig. 4)

Teeth may be blackened out by drying the tooth with tissue and coloring it with black eyebrow pencil.

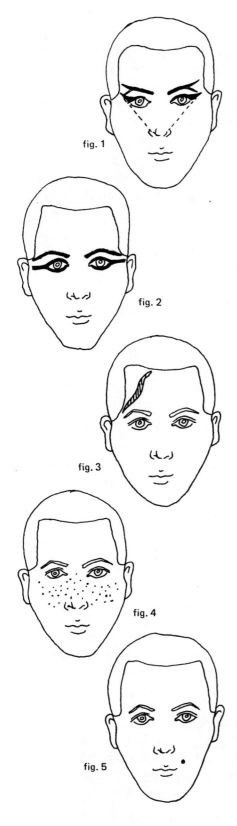

fig. 1

fig. 2

fig. 3

fig. 4

fig. 5

White shoe polish touched lightly on hair makes a graying effect. So does powder but powder has a way of puffing away in the breeze.

Make bushy hair by back combing. Bushy eyebrows are made by combing the brows in the wrong direction.

Lips grow thinner through the years. For extreme age, color them with foundation to match the rest of the face. If lipstick is needed, use beige.

MORE SPECIAL EFFECTS

Oriental eyes — With black eyeliner, starting at the inner corner next to the lashes, draw a line that sweeps across the eyelid and upward. The end should sweep from a 45 degree angle with the outer corner of the nostril. Eyebrows should tilt slightly, too, at the same angle. (See fig. 1)

Egyptian eyes — Line heavily with black eyeliner from inner corner extending beyond outer corner to temple. Lower lid line should meet upper lid line at outer corner. (See fig.2)

Diseases — Measles, rashes, sunburn and red blotches can be made with rouge or clown red make-up, or, in a pinch, with red lipstick blended lightly.

For leprosy, paint white blotches with white shoe polish or clown white make-up. Accent with outlines around the blotches in brown eyebrow pencil. Contrast the pale, scaly skin with dark shadows under the eyes and hollow cheeks.

Wounds — Draw a gash with an eyebrow pencil. Fill in with red lipstick. (See fig. 3)

Freckles — Touch an eyebrow pencil to any freckles that are already there, mostly across the nose and cheekbones. For comic effect, make them big and round. (See fig. 4)

Beauty marks — With a blunt eyebrow pencil, put the point of the pencil on the skin and twirl it. This should make a perfect circle. (See fig. 5)

BEARDS

fig. 1

These are typical Near Eastern beard styles. Crepe hair is stuck to the face in small strips with spirit gum or latex. Apply the hair in the direction hair grows. (See fig. 1) The art of beard creation requires practice. After the hair is stuck to the whole area needed for the beard, trim the shape desired with scissors.

Crepe hair comes in braided ropes which have to be unbraided, wet, and pressed between two towels with a warm iron. It comes in several colors. For best results, blend two colors such as brown and black. One color tends to look more artificial when used alone.

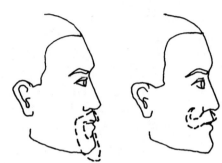

Latex is the best adhesive for beards because it can be peeled off and used over and over. Follow directions on the label of the jar.

Spirit gum looks like school glue and is painted on. Use a one inch brush and paint small sections at one time or it will dry before you can get hair on. It is a messy process at best but the results can be worth it. Whichever method you use, experiment and practice.

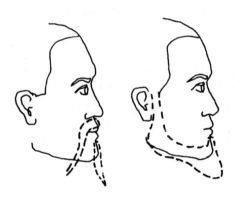

Crepe hair has a way of itching and it has been known to fall off when you least want it to if it isn't put on properly. For these reasons, it is preferable to grow your own beard, if possible.

A little beard goes a long way so don't be tempted to make everyone look like Santa Claus. It is nice to have someone specialize in beards, particularly since Bible plays require so many.

When only a tiny beard or moustache is required and close inspection isn't going to happen, it can be painted on with good old eyebrow pencil or liner. Powder over it to prevent shine.

CARE AND STORAGE OF MAKE-UP

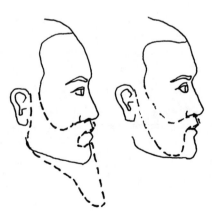

Collect shoe boxes and plastic bags for storage. Another good idea is the fisherman's tackle box with all of its compartments. The bigger the better, of course. If everyone is to have his own set of make-up, give each their own box of supplies with whatever he/she needs. Usually it works out that most of the actors can put on their basic make-up and two or three specialists take care of every-one's special effects. This is a happy arrangement, especially with beards and complicated effects.

Ideally, the company should have a room with lots of tables, chairs and mirrors where they can make up without tripping over each other or waiting in line.

After each performance all things should be cleaned, caps replaced, lids closed, pencils sharpened, empties refilled, and anything else made ready for the next performance. Cosmetics must be stored away from heat or they will melt or evaporate. The room is likely to be a mess after a performance so it will need to be straightened. All the straightening and organizing you do will pay off when you want to find something in a hurry. And, that is practically all the time.

Little Kid's Theater—Not for the Faint-hearted

If you love working with preschoolers and slightly older children,
you know what fun it is and how hard it is to come up with ideas they enjoy doing.
No sitting still for them. "Playing" plays is ideal for that age because it keeps
them doing what they love to do—play pretend. If you supply the read-aloud
story for them, it gives them whole plots, more elaborate and more structured
than they can construct for themselves.

I developed my method from watching how the little ones played. First, they
assign themselves roles (I'll be the mommy and you be the daddy). Then they
invent or elaborate on an incident (Let's pretend we are going to the store). They
work out who is going to do what and what each will say: (Pretend I said....and
you said....). Then they do that much and stop to work out another episode in
the same way.

After watching a group of four-year-olds playing one day, I wondered if they'd like
some help. So I read a story to them and paused to let them repeat the dialog
and act out the movements. As I thought, they loved having actions and dialog
"fed" to them. After that experiment, I picked out storybooks with lots of dialog
and characters; then I divided the text into short sequences, marking places to
stop so the children could act out what had happened in the narrative. I read the
dialog to them one sentence at a time and waited while they repeated their lines.

Not only would the children get naturally into character but they would repeat the
lines exactly as I gave them. We were no longer reading lines but acting.

This method of fitting a story around the way children naturally play worked so
incredibly well that we formed a class.

What the children thought was just play time became rehearsal time (to me) so
that before long we had shows to perform. Children who couldn't read were
memorizing pages of dialog without even being told to. Repetition was all they
needed. In the beginning, they repeated the lines after the narrator. After a few
times, all the narrator had to say was "he said" and the little actors would take it
from there.

As for the acting, children hardly need lessons from adults. They are natural
mimics and performing comes as naturally as breathing for most of them. Even
shy children can't resist getting into the act.

The main job of the director is to block out the action and keep control of stage movements so that the action flows smoothly from place to place. It helps to have both a narrator and director, but one person can do both in a pinch.

How easy can it be?

- Before any acting takes place, read the story to the class so that they know what to expect. Have a supply of props ready too.

- Assign parts.

- Block out locations according to scenes. (Here is the house, there is the garden, etc.) The actors will need some help in the beginning to know where to go when movement is required.

- Hand out props. The kids just have to have props. That's what toys are, after all.

- Now the teacher or narrator begins re-reading the story, pausing to let the actors mime the action as it occurs. The reader feeds their speeches to the players one line at a time. Show them how the lines should be said with emphasis and emotion—act, don't just read.

- Actors repeat their lines. (You'll be amazed how well!)

- After a few repetitions, actors will begin to know their lines and the play starts to come together.

If you've come this far, you may as well add costumes and give a performance! Even if kids get stage fright and make mistakes, the parents will love it.

Our first performance was a riot. The audience loved it but they laughed and scared the children half to death. Prepare the children for audience reactions. Children need to be told that if the audience laughs it is with delight and encouragement—not because the audience is making fun.